Jesus and the Word:

It's a Package Deal

By Karen Todd

New Harbor Press
RAPID CITY, SD

Copyright © 2022 by Karen Todd.

All rights reserved. No part of this publication may be reproduced, distributed or transmitted in any form or by any means, including photocopying, recording, or other electronic or mechanical methods, without the prior written permission of the publisher, except in the case of brief quotations embodied in critical reviews and certain other noncommercial uses permitted by copyright law. For permission requests, write to the publisher, addressed "Attention: Permissions Coordinator," at the address below.

Todd/New Harbor Press
1601 Mt.Rushmore Rd, Ste 3288
Rapid City, SD 57701
www.newharborpress.com

Ordering Information:
Quantity sales. Special discounts are available on quantity purchases by corporations, associations, and others. For details, contact the "Special Sales Department" at the address above.

Jesus and the Word: It's a Package Deal / Karen Todd. —1st ed.
ISBN 978-1-63357-263-8

Scripture quotations marked "TLB" are taken from the Living Bible copyright © 1971 by Tyndale House Foundation. Used by permission of Tyndale House Publishers Inc., Carol Stream, Illinois 60188. All rights reserved.

Scripture quotations marked "NIV" are taken from the Holy Bible, New International Version®, NIV®. Copyright © 1973, 1978, 1984, 2011 by Biblica, Inc.™ Used by permission of Zondervan. All rights reserved worldwide. www.zondervan.com The "NIV" and "New International Version" are trademarks registered in the United States Patent and Trademark Office by Biblica, Inc.™

Scripture quotations marked "KJV" are taken from the Holy Bible, King James Version (Public Domain).

Preface

THIS BOOK IS WRITTEN for anyone and everyone! Whether you are a Christian, and are struggling through some valleys, or someone who has never known Jesus. Perhaps you are someone who thinks you are not worthy of Christ's love because of things you may have done previously. There is nothing that can keep Jesus from forgiving you and loving you. My hope is that you will read this and know how much Jesus loves you! You are His child, and He is waiting on YOU!

Contents

[1] Introduction 3

[2] Background Story 7

[3] The Turning Point 13

[4] Be Not Afraid and Speak Up 17

[5] Old Testament / New Testament 21

[6] God's Word / A Plan for Living 25

[7] Let the Holy Spirit Guide You 29

[8] The Stubborn and Prideful 31

[9] Experiencing Knowing Christ 35

[10] Do Not Be Quiet 39

[11] The Things of This World 41

[12] Jesus First / We Are Second 45

[13] He Is Where Our Help Comes From 53

[14] Be Prepared 57

[15] Oh, Holy Spirit Come 61

[16] Experiencing Baptism 65

[17] Three in One 69

[18] Personal Experiences 73

[19] Choosing Jesus 77

[1]

INTRODUCTION

WELL, I HAVE FINALLY had it! This is it, the last straw, **the final turning point** so to speak, and the reason that sparked my intention to write this book in the first place. I will share this final turning point with you further into the book, but this is how I know in my heart that this world, God's creation, is truly struggling and that we need all the help we can get. Before, it had always been that I knew that some people were Christians and maybe some weren't. There are so many "religions" in today's time that I literally think, "Wow, what must God be feeling and thinking!" But now, after witnessing what some people (who have supposedly been saved and are Christians) seem to believe, I realize what a huge part of the problem is or, at least, what I believe is a huge part of the problem. First, I will introduce myself, as I am sure that you want to know just exactly who I am, so that you may relate to me in a better way.

Who am I? I'm no one really any different than anyone else. I am simply a woman who has lived through many hills and valleys as most people have, and I will refer to *hills* as the positive and/or bright parts of my life and *valleys* as the low parts of my life. We all have them. I am a daughter, sister, mother, aunt, sister-in-law, grandmother, cousin, niece, and friend to multiple people. I have held many positions during my precollege years, college years, and postcollege years. I have been a lifeguard, student and athlete, an employee with college work study programs, and an employee of several businesses throughout these years. I have been a Sunday school teacher, Bible school teacher, youth sports coach, tutor, and a teacher for the past nineteen years in some form in the public school system. These positions have put me in many different surroundings, some more positive than others, but each provided me with some type of learning experience. I have only recently decided to discontinue my career as a teacher. I have raised my own children who are all grown adults now and have enjoyed it tremendously despite the valleys that fell between the hills. I say all of this to show that my life isn't much different than yours. We all struggle with jobs, family, friends, and life in general which is what makes us all the same. However, having Christ with us through all these struggles does make the difference.

Psalm 23:4—Yea, when I walk through the valley of the shadows, I will fear no evil

Psalm 72:3—Let the mountains bring peace to the people, and the hills, in righteousness

But, of all the titles that I have held, the one I cherish the most is being a child of God. This is what has enabled me to get through the valleys and to appreciate the hills.

[2]

BACKGROUND STORY

GOD IS WITH EACH of us, and He is committed to us during all times, not just during the hills. While experiencing a valley, we will eventually begin to grow out of that valley with the help of the Lord once we have given our life to Him. Over time, I have really matured and grown in my walk with the Lord, so much so, that I have continued to have a desire to bring others to know Him. I went from going to Sunday school when I was at a young age, to being confirmed in church at age eleven, then, only went occasionally throughout high school and college. Then, during my years of marriage, eighteen to be exact, I began to be a devout regular at Sunday school and church where I enjoyed learning and reading God's Word. Since, I have realized that it is not the denomination that matters; but it is the asking and accepting of Jesus Christ in your heart as your Lord and Savior and repenting of your sins that matters and, then, walking the best you can in God's Word.

After eighteen years of being married, *tragedy* struck, and our family experienced divorce. For me, I call this a tragedy. I was distraught. I cried every night for what seemed like an eternity. I would wait until my kids were all asleep and then let the tears flow. I'm sure I thought the same thing that many others thought. "What is happening? I can't believe this . . . ." This wasn't a part of the plan. This was something that I did not believe in, and it was devastating to me. Yet, it happened.

I made a move to better my finances in some way, at least, so that I could take care of my kids in the best way possible. Again, the Lord stepped in and provided for me a job and, to this day, I give Him all the praise for that. You see, I had no connections to help me get this job and not much experience, yet I was hired over 100 applicants. There was no other explanation for this miracle.

This was when the churchgoing stopped. In my head, I was saying it was because no one from the previous church reached out to me or my kids during this difficult time after we had known these people for so long. I thought, "Really? These people are Christians?" This was probably the first thing that put a question in my mind about people who say they are Christians and have been saved. This was absolutely no excuse, but, every time I mentioned going to church, no one wanted to go. My kids were middle school age and older, and looking back, I know I should have tried to make them attend church, but I was picking and choosing my battles. Well, that should have been the one I chose.

However, this did not affect my Christian walk. In fact, I knew that I had to continue to reassure my kids that this was not God's doing at all. I continued to keep Christ in our home with the usual prayers and in conversations. I never hesitated to share Christian views and beliefs within our home when issues or topics arose. This was a huge and difficult valley for me and my kids. Yet, God was always there with me throughout every difficult moment. This only strengthened my walk with Jesus.

Joshua 1:9—Have I not commanded you? Be strong and courageous. Do not be frightened, and do not be dismayed, for the Lord your God is with you wherever you go.

I spent lots of one-on-one time with Jesus and God, saying prayers and thanking Him for many blessings that I still had in my life. Over the next ten years, I would have to say that I experienced as many hills as valleys, and I celebrated those hills and just kept on going through those valleys, but always being hopeful.

Throughout my teaching career, I have always kept an open Bible on my desk, which most would say I was crazy to do. Having God's Word on my desk was never questioned, believe it or not, and I feel like He was always there, not letting anything or anyone keep me from having it. In fact, having the Bible there prompted many conversations with others, both adults and students. I once had a maintenance worker come in my classroom after school to fix the light in one of the ceiling tiles, and he saw my Bible. He said it was the first time he had ever seen a Bible in a classroom, and he was amazed that I had it out and open on my desk but was happy to see it. My students have always seen my love for Jesus and have openly talked about it with me. When all my own kids were out of school, I began to watch sermons on television and online, and I realized how much I missed learning and listening to the Word. I mean, I had always continued praying steadily over the years as well as reading my Bible verse books, but I had not submerged myself in the Word. I then began attending church regularly, as well as reading God's Word daily.

As I said, over the years, there have been many hills and valleys, and Jesus has been the one steady constant in my life through all of them, my rock, always there, always hearing my prayers, and always finding a way to work things out. I wondered, "How do people in these tough situations make it through without Him?" It just cannot be done on your own. You see, people in general will say, "Get over it," but God doesn't say get over it. He simply guides you as you continue to move forward and is always there to help you and support you with His love and strength.

Hebrews 13:15—Keep your life free from love of money, and be content with what you have, for he has said, I will never leave you nor forsake you.

Matthew 6:25–34—Therefore I tell you, do not worry about your life, what you will eat or drink; or about your body, what you will wear. Is not life more than food, and the body more than clothes? Look at the birds of the air; they do not sow or reap or store away in barns, and yet your heavenly Father feeds them. Are you not much more valuable than they; Can anyone of you by worrying add a single hour to your life? And why do you worry about clothes; See how the flowers of the field grow. They do not labor or spin. Yet I tell you that not even Solomon in all his splendor was dressed like one of these. If that is how God clothes the grass of the field, which is here today and tomorrow is thrown into the fire, will he not much more clothe you—you of little faith? So do not worry, saying, "What shall we eat?" Or "What shall we drink?" or "What shall we wear?" For the Pagans run after all these things, and your heavenly Father knows that you need them. But seek first His kingdom and His righteousness, and all these things will be given to you as well. Therefore, do not worry about tomorrow, for tomorrow will worry about itself. Each day has enough trouble of its own.

[3]

THE TURNING POINT

I HAVE TAUGHT MANY students over these past years and have seen many former students become very successful, both in their professions and in their Christian walk. However, there have also been others who have strayed in their walk with Christ and/or have not come to know the Lord at all. It makes my heart hurt to see this. Please, do not think that my family is immune to this hurt. We also have those who have strayed from Christ. This world is a tough one and there are constant battles throughout each day for all people, whether they admit it or not.

But here it is, the thing that finally got to me, **that so called turning point** I mentioned at the beginning. Many students that I have known to be faithful in their Christian walk and faithful in their Christian Church Youth groups, always talking the talk of knowing Christ, and receiving Christ as their Savior, are also the very same people who did not choose to minister to others when the opportunity presented itself.

When their very closest friends strayed from Jesus, instead of ministering to them about Jesus, they assured their lost friends that it was okay to be involved in the things that they were doing, even though God's Word clearly states the opposite. They told their friends that, if they had accepted Christ as their Savior, it was okay. Mostly, I believe that this is about friends not wanting to lose friendships. In all honesty, to be a real friend means being able to say what you believe and standing on your faith. I was amazed by the number of people in this world today who don't truly know the Word of God, but say they have accepted Christ as their Savior. "How can there be one without the other I asked myself?" They go together. Either you believe in all of God's Word, or you don't. There is no in-between.

John 1:1—In the beginning was the Word, and the Word was with God, and the Word was God.

This verse itself states the same words spoken in Genesis 1:1. Both begin with "In the beginning." This is showing that Christ was present in the Creation, even though he had not been born of Mary yet. Jesus is not only the Word, but He is the creator as well, one with God. People who do not really know Jesus are often those who do not know the Word as well. **Jesus and the Word are one and the same!**

I believe that is why there are so many confused Christians. Most of these people state that, if you've accepted Christ as your Savior, it's okay to do what you want. Therefore, a lot of people listen to their friends and continue to live a sinful life, not even realizing they are sinning daily, and there is no repentance involved. How confusing this must be to so many individuals! The whole reason behind repenting of your sins and asking Jesus to be your Savior and Lord, is that you will receive forgiveness for your sins, and your heart will be changed forever. Because of this change, a person has no desire to continue those sinful ways and will commit to not making those same choices. They literally feel different and new! This is the reason it is called being "born again" in Christ. Even though we all sin, when we are truly saved, we feel bad about it and repent and then start back over and try to live more like Christ. Many of these people do not feel this way, and it saddens me. I'm wondering, "Are they really saved?" or "Are they pushing back against the Holy Spirit?"

1 John 3:9—No one born of God makes a practice of sinning, for God's seed abides in him, and he cannot keep on sinning because he has been born of God

2 Corinthians 5:17—Therefore, if there is anyone in Christ, the new creation has come: The old has gone, the new is here!

I'm also wondering how much of God's Word they have read or studied. Do they just listen to what their so-called friends tell them? These are usually the people that do not mind if their friends continue along their strayed paths. Also, the ones who have strayed refuse to go to church or sit and visit with a pastor, other than the one that is condoning their behavior. And yes, there are pastors today who will condone certain behaviors instead of really relying on God's Word and the Holy Spirit. It's really heartbreaking. Some of these more popular, deceiving comments refer to what the Old Testament says about certain things. My goodness! So many people do not understand the difference between the Old Testament and the New Testament or even the Gospel and what it represents. Again, I am not even a pastor, but I can only imagine the confusion that is in our world. Many people use this lack of knowledge for the reasoning behind the choices they are making. It's like an excuse from that lack of knowledge.

[4]

BE NOT AFRAID AND SPEAK UP

1 CORINTHIANS 6:9–10—DO YOU not know that the unrighteous will not inherit the kingdom of God? Do not be deceived. Neither fornicators, nor idolaters, nor adulterers, nor homosexuals, nor Sodomites will have a share in His Kingdom.

Notice that nowhere in the verse above does it say not to love all people. There is total confusion in this phrase that is out in the world today. That is why Jesus said, "Love first." He did not say, "Agree first." It is okay to disagree and have different beliefs about things, but you can still love someone. In today's world, it is mainly stated that you can't love someone if you disagree with them about what they are doing. That is just not true!

Sometimes, all people really need is to hear the Gospel Truth and the New Testament from a close friend to, at least, possibly prompt them to consider learning more about the Word. Other times, it may be a total stranger that shares this news. That is why it is so important for us to reach out to others and share the Gospel. Most of the time, people who stray from their walk with Jesus will not listen to their own family, the people who truly love and care about them second to Jesus. If they have a very close friend, then, they may be able to talk with them. It is very sad to see friends condone what their other friends are doing, if they know it is not godly in the eyes of the Lord.

I also believe in this crazy world today, which can also be enjoyed thoroughly while walking with Jesus, that people are too afraid to say it like it is, instead of just coming out and addressing the issues whatever they may be. I'm totally not comparing one sin to another because sin is sin. However, this is where people get offended if "their sin" is addressed or questioned. Maybe the sin is lying to others, stealing, having same-sex relations, committing adultery, pornography, murdering, raping, changing your sexuality, etc. Each of these sins is a choice, with not one being greater than another. However, they are choices. You can find individuals everywhere that have chosen Jesus over any of these desires. That being the case, it is a choice as those people will tell you. No one said it would be easy, but with Jesus on your side, it is possible, and He will make a way for you.

Matthew 7:21–23—Not everyone who says to me, "Lord, Lord," will enter the kingdom of heaven, but the one who does the will of my Father who is in heaven. On that day, many will say to me, "Lord, did we not prophesy in your name, and cast out demons in your name, and do many mighty works in your name?" And then will I declare to them, "I never knew you; depart from me, you workers of lawlessness."

James 4:4—You adulterous people, don't you know that friendship with the world means enmity against God? Therefore, anyone who chooses to be a friend of the world becomes an enemy of God.

Romans 6:1–12—So do you think we should continue sinning, so that God will give us more and more grace? Of course not! Our old sinful life ended. It's dead. So how can we continue living in sin? Did you forget that all of us became part of Christ Jesus when we were baptized? In our baptism, we shared in his death. So, when we were baptized, we were buried with Christ and took part in his death. And just as Christ was raised from death by the wonderful power of the Father, so we can now live a new life. Christ died, and we have been joined with him by dying too. So, we will also be joined with him by rising from death as he did. We know that our old life was put to death on the cross with Christ. This happened, so that our sinful selves would have no power over us. Then we would not be slaves to sin. Anyone who has died is made free from sin's control. If we died with Christ, we know that we will also live with him. Christ was raised from death, and we know that he cannot die again. Death has no power over him now. Yes, when Christ died, he died to defeat the power of sin one time—enough for all time. He now has a new life, and his new life is with God. In the same way, you should see yourselves as being dead to the power of sin and alive for God through Christ Jesus. But don't let sin control your life here on Earth. You must not be ruled by the things your sinful self makes you want to do.

1 John 3:6—No one who lives in Him keeps on sinning. No one who continues to sin has either seen Him or known Him.

[5]

OLD TESTAMENT / NEW TESTAMENT

MOSES BROUGHT US THE Law in the Old Testament. But that law brought us sin and death. This was meant to make us ready for the coming of Jesus. If you are under the Old Testament Law, then you will continue to sin and that's exactly what Satan wants you to do. He wants you to try to stay under that Law and not move to Christ. Jesus came in the New Testament and brought us grace, so that we could repent and be saved through Christ's name and live eternally with God. He did not come to give us grace, so that we would continue to repeat those sins.

Galatians 5:19–21—Now the works of the flesh are manifest, which are these; Adultery, fornication, uncleanness, lasciviousness (lustfulness), idolatry, witchcraft, hatred, variance, emulations, wrath, strife, seditions, heresies, envyings, murders, drunkenness, revellings, and such like: of the which I tell you before, as I have also told you in time past, that they which do such things shall not inherit the kingdom of God.

Luke 6:46—And why call me Lord, Lord, and do not do the things that I say?

The Laws of the Old Testament were not meant to bring about or earn salvation!

Galatians 3:11—But that no man is justified by the law in the sight of God, it is evident: for, the just shall live by faith.

Those laws were simply intended to lead us to Christ in the future, so that we would gain salvation through grace. The ritual laws from the Old Testament concerning sacrifice, priesthood, and the Temple are no longer a part of the church, because Jesus came and replaced them. So many young people are being told otherwise and believe so much of the Old Testament over the Gospel because that is what they are told by the company they keep. Again, this is their reasoning for choosing wrongful sins and believing it is okay, or, that it's "just how they are." AND . . . because so many do not speak up about it and pretend that they are okay with it, that makes it seem perfectly fine, when in truth it is not. Please understand, the entire Word of God is true and factual, but Jesus came in the New Testament to discontinue the laws of the Old Testament.

God's favor cannot be won by following old laws, and it cannot be won by doing good deeds. You can't save yourself. Only Jesus can do this when you commit to Him by faith through grace.

Ephesians 2:8–9—For by grace you have been saved through faith and this is not your own doing; it is a gift of God, not a result of works, so that no one may boast.

[6]

God's Word / A Plan for Living

ALL OF THIS IS to remind you how important it is to learn and study God's Word. It is truly God's Word that shows us how to live.

2 Timothy 3:16–17—All Scripture is inspired by God and is useful to teach us what is true and to make us realize what is wrong in our lives. It corrects us when we are wrong and teaches us to do what is right. God uses it to prepare and equip His people to do every good work.

Hebrews 4:12—For the Word of God is quick, and powerful, and sharper than any two-edged sword, piercing even to the dividing asunder of soul and spirit, and of the joints and marrow, and is a discerner of the thoughts and intents of the heart.

Luke 11:28—But he said, Yea rather, blessed are they that hear the word of God, and keep it.

John 1:1—In the beginning was the Word, and the Word was with God, and the Word was God.

Psalm 119:11—Thy word have I hid in mine heart, that I might not sin against thee.

Do these people who say they are Christians even know what the Word says? Do they understand that when the word *bread* is used, it is referring to the Word of God, which nourishes the crowds spiritually and means "sharing," and not always the bread that we physically eat? I wonder. Do they understand that the old laws of eating pork, etc. are just that? OLD! The new has come with Christ. If I hear another young adult say that eating pork is a sin, I may really preach the Word for hours and, again, I am not even a pastor but just an average person like everyone else.

God's Word also tells us how we can protect ourselves from the worldly ways in today's time. I would like to believe that the answer is always, "The devil made you do it," but, ultimately, it is a person's choice to follow their pride and flesh which is what Satan wants them to do. I mean, after all, Satan's sole purpose is to separate as many people as possible from God the Father. God's Word tells us how to fight against these worldly things.

Ephesians 6:11–18—Put on the full armor of God, so that you can take your stand against the devil's schemes. For our struggle is not against other's flesh and blood, but against the rulers, against the authorities, against the powers of the dark world and against the spiritual forces of evil in the heavenly realms. Therefore, put on the full armor of God, so that when the day of evil comes, you may be able to stand your ground, and after you've done everything, to stand. Stand firm then, with the belt of truth buckled around your waist, with the breastplate of righteousness in place, and with your feet fitted with the readiness that comes from the Gospel of peace. In addition to all this, take up the shield of faith, with which you can extinguish all the flaming arrows of the evil one. Take the helmet of salvation and the sword of the Spirit, which is the Word of God. And pray in the Spirit on all occasions with all kinds of prayers and requests and with this in mind, be alert, and always keep on praying for all the Lord's people.

The thing is, even though this world has deteriorated in a lot of ways, there are so many good things still out there that we, as God's children, can enjoy. If more people would truly commit to the Word of God, what a change there could be! Obviously, when we are aware of a person who is struggling in their walk with Christ, or they haven't accepted Christ as their Lord and Savior, it is our job to love them and minister to them. The problem is that, most of the time, these people refuse to listen if it isn't what they want to hear.

John 17:24—Father, I want those you have given me to be with me where I am, and to see my glory, the glory you have given me, because you loved me before the creation of the world.

[7]

LET THE HOLY SPIRIT GUIDE YOU

REASSURE OTHERS THAT WHEN Christ died for our sins and rose again to sit at the right hand of God the Father, He sent the Holy Spirit to be with us here on Earth, to dwell inside of us. Once you've received grace through Christ, the Holy Spirit begins to help you change. The Holy Spirit can reshape your desires! Don't let sin define you, but let Jesus define you! Your behavior and sin can dictate you, so hold on to who you are in Jesus Christ. Grace is your way out of sin. The Holy Spirit can bring you to a point where your sin is not a temptation to you anymore.

Romans 8:5–6—Those who live according to the flesh have their minds set on what the flesh desires; but those who live in accordance with the Spirit have their minds set on what the Spirit desires. The mind governed by the flesh is death, but the mind governed by the Spirit is life and peace.

John 14:26—But the Advocate, the Holy Spirit, whom the Father will send in my name, will teach you all things and will remind you of everything I have said to you.

Acts 2:38—Peter replied, "Repent and be baptized, every one of you, in the name of Jesus Christ for the forgiveness of your sins. And you will receive the gift of the Holy Spirit."

Romans 8:26—In the same way, the Spirit helps us in our weakness. We do not know what we ought to pray for, but the Spirit himself intercedes for us through wordless groans.

You see now that accepting Jesus Christ as your Lord and Savior and repenting of your sins will get you grace, a free gift that is received through faith in Christ, and the Holy Spirit will be forever within your heart.

[8]

THE STUBBORN AND PRIDEFUL

THIS REPENTING OF SINS seems to also be misunderstood by many. To repent is to not be greater than God Himself, but on the contrary, one must humble himself before the Lord totally and completely and ask to be forgiven for his/her sins. This is a struggle for some who have strong personalities and are full of pride. To surrender one's whole self to the Lord Jesus, and ask for forgiveness of your sins (you must know the Word to know that you are sinning), is very difficult indeed for some, because those who are full of pride tend to think that it makes them weak to do this.

Romans 2:5—But because of your stubbornness and unrepenting heart, you are storing up wrath against yourself for the day of God's wrath, when His righteous judgement will be revealed.

Romans 12:2—Do not conform to the pattern of this world but be transformed by the renewing of your mind. Then you will be able to test and approve what God's will is—his good, pleasing and perfect will.

1 Samuel 16:7—But the Lord said to Samuel, "Don't judge by his appearance or height, for I have rejected him. The Lord doesn't see things the way you see them. People judge by outward appearance, but the Lord looks at the heart."

1 John 2:15–17—Do not love the world or anything in the world. If anyone loves the world, love for the Father is not in them. For everything in the world—the lust of the flesh, the lust of the eyes, and the pride of life—comes not from the Father but from the world. The world and its desires pass away, but whoever does the will of God lives forever.

Proverbs 3:34—Towards the scorners, He is scornful, but to the humble he gives favor.

1 Peter 5:5—Likewise, you who are younger, be subject to the elders. Clothe yourselves, all of you, with humility toward one another, for "God opposes the proud but gives grace to the humble."

Philippians 2:3—Do nothing from selfish ambition or conceit, but in humility count others more significant than yourselves.

Proverbs 16:18—Pride goes before destruction, and a haughty spirit before a fall.

James 4:6—But He gives more grace. Therefore, it says, "God opposes the proud but gives grace to the humble."

Proverbs 16:5—Everyone who is arrogant in heart is an abomination to the Lord; be assured, he will not go unpunished.

As you can see, there are many verses in God's Word that speak of the prideful. But, when one can truly surrender his/herself to Christ and admit that He is strong and they are weak, and then tell Christ that you need Him each second of every minute, of every hour, of every day, that is when you are humbled, and Jesus will bless you in ways you've never known!

Matthew 5:6— "Blessed are those who hunger and thirst for righteousness, for they shall be satisfied."

Luke 5:32—I have not come to call the righteous but the sinners to repentance.

Acts 3:19— "Now repent of your sins and turn to God, so that your sins may be wiped away."

[9]

EXPERIENCING KNOWING CHRIST

ONE THING THAT I can tell you is that, once a person begins to read the Scriptures, they will continue to be drawn to them. And, once someone has truly given their life to Christ, they will know, because there will be a joy they have never experienced, a joy that will surpass any other. There will be a burning desire to share their love for Christ and witness to others. They will want to experience God's Word in every way. They will want to try their best to live as Christ and, even though they may fall short of doing this, they will repent and feel remorseful when they do sin and, then, they will start all over again and try to do better the next day.

Romans 3:23—For all have sinned; we all fall short of God's glorious standard.

With Christ helping us and the Holy Spirit fighting for us, we will continue to grow stronger in our faith and help others come to know Christ as well.

John 14:14–17—If you ask me anything in my name, I will do it. If you love me, you will keep my commandments. And I will ask the Father, and He will give you another Helper, to be with you forever, even the Spirit of truth, whom the world cannot receive, because it neither sees Him nor knows Him. You know Him, for He dwells with you and will be in you.

Whenever you experience a valley, just know that God has a reason, a plan, that only He knows about, and we must trust in that plan. Use that valley to help others when they find themselves in a valley. We all have valleys and hills, but we are called to share the Gospel with everyone we can. I am now convinced more than ever, that so many in the world today need to know the meaning of God's Word and the importance of it in our lives. Instead, the world has picked out parts of the Word to believe and disregards other parts depending on what that person wants to believe. It's impossible to do that. God's Word is steadfast, and it will still be here long after all the things of this world are gone. The Word will remain the same, and it will still be the voice of truth.

God's Word reminds us that accepting Christ as our Savior and repenting go hand in hand.

Leviticus 18:4—You shall follow my rules and keep my statutes and walk in them. I am the Lord your God.

John 10:4—When He has brought out all of His own, He goes before them, and the sheep follow Him, for they know His voice.

Deuteronomy 13:4—Serve only the Lord your God and fear Him alone. Obey his commands, listen to His voice, and cling to Him.

Isaiah 48:17—This is what the Lord says—your Redeemer, the Holy One of Israel: I am the Lord your God, who teaches you what is good for you and leads you along the paths you should follow.

1 Samuel 12:14—Now if you fear and worship the Lord and listen to His voice, and if you do not rebel against the Lord's commands, then both you and your king will show that you recognize the Lord as your God.

[10]

Do Not Be Quiet

SO PLEASE, PLEASE, HELP all of those who are lost in this world find the light of Jesus. Don't be afraid to stand on your faith and reach out to them teaching them the Word.

1 Peter 3:15—But in your hearts, honor Christ the Lord as holy, always being prepared to make a defense to anyone who asks you for a reason for the hope that is in you; yet do it with gentleness and respect.

Mark 16:15–16—And He said to them, "Go into all the world and proclaim the gospel to the whole creation. Whoever believes and is baptized will be saved, but whoever does not believe will be condemned."

Romans 10:13–14—For everyone who calls on the name of the Lord will be saved. How then will they call on Him in whom they have not believed? And how are they to believe in Him of whom they have never heard? And how are they to hear without someone preaching?

John 14:6—Jesus said to him, "I am the way, and the truth, and the life. No one comes to the Father except through me."

Galatians 6:9—So let's not get tired of doing what is good. At just the right time we will reap a harvest of blessing if we don't give up.

Psalm 96:3—Declare His glory among the nations, His marvelous works among all the peoples!

Matthew 28:19–20—Go therefore and make disciples of all nations, baptizing them in the name of the Father, and of the Son, and of the Holy Spirit, teaching them to observe all that I have commanded you; and lo, I am with you always, to the close of the age.

James 5:19–20—My brothers and sisters, if one of you should wander from the truth and someone should bring that person back, remember this: Whoever turns a sinner from the error of their way will save them from death and cover over a multitude of sins.

Philemon 1:6—and I pray that the sharing of your faith may become effective for the full knowledge of every good thing that is in us for the sake of Christ.

[11]

THE THINGS OF THIS WORLD

THIS WORLD TODAY IS all about "things," money, social media, what feels good to the flesh, etc. The thing is, there are places in this world where all these things fit, but only when connected to Christ. For instance, social media can be used for good and can be Christlike to share joy with others. However, everyone knows that this is not the case for the most part. In fact, it is another way that Satan attacks us. Satan himself doesn't do it, as Satan has already been defeated by Jesus, as it states in the New Testament.

Luke 4:1–13—Jesus, full of the Holy Spirit, returned from the Jordan and was led by the Spirit in the desert, where for forty days he was tempted by the devil. He ate nothing during those days, and at the end of them he was hungry. The devil said to him,

"If you are the Son of God, tell this stone to become bread." Jesus answered, "It is written, man does not live on bread alone." The devil led him up to a high place and showed him in an instant all the kingdom. And he said to him, "I will give you all their authority and splendor, for it has been given to me, and I can give it to anyone I want to. So, if you worship me, it will all be yours." Jesus answered, "It is written: 'Worship the Lord your God and serve him only.'" The devil led him to Jerusalem and had him stand on the highest point of the temple. "If you are the Son of God," he said, "throw yourself down from here. For it is written: 'He will command his angels concerning you to guard you carefully; they will lift you up in their hands, so that you will not strike your foot against a stone.'" Jesus answered, "It says: Do not put the Lord your God to the test."

Thus, Jesus defeated Satan for good. However, people choose to use social media inappropriately and in a negative manner. This thrills Satan! You see, Jesus doesn't care how many Instagram followers you have or how many retweets, likes, or loves that you get on your social media. That means absolutely nothing to Him. On Judgment Day, God will not be asking you about those kinds of things. He will be recounting all the things in your life that you have done and said and all the things you could have been doing. Make no mistake, you will be judged by every word and deed.

2 Corinthians 11:13–15—For such men are false apostles, deceitful workmen, disguising themselves as apostles of Christ. And no wonder, for even Satan disguises himself as an angel of light. So, it is no surprise if his servants, also, disguise themselves as servants of righteousness. Their end will correspond to their deeds.

John 12:48— "But, all who reject me and my message will be judged on the day of judgement by the truth I have spoken."

Psalm 23:1–6—The Lord is my shepherd; I shall not want. He makes me lie down in green pastures. He leads me beside still waters. He restores my soul. He leads me in paths of righteousness for His name's sake. Even though I walk through the valley of the shadow of death, I will fear no evil, for you are with me; your rod and your staff, they comfort me. You prepare a table before me in the presence of my enemies; you anoint my head with oil; my cup overflows. Surely goodness and mercy shall follow me all the days of my life, and I shall dwell in the house of the Lord forever.

2 Corinthians 4:4—Satan, who is the God of "this world," has blinded the minds of those who don't believe. They are unable to see the glorious light of

the Good News. They don't understand this message about the glory of Christ, who is the exact likeness of God.

[12]

JESUS FIRST / WE ARE SECOND

IN THIS NEXT PART, I will share the truth about this whole idea of "do what feels good to the flesh," as it is also addressed in God's Word. It saddens me that so many leaders in our present "church world," whatever the denomination may be, have continually began to condone this state of mind. It is okay to disagree! Like I said before, I am not an expert in any way, shape, or form, but I would have to say it is surprising about those who are continuing to try to preach the Gospel but not having courage to stand up for God's Word. Now, don't misunderstand me, there are still many church leaders that do stand up for their faith and the Word, but it's the others that do not that have promoted this idea of "do what feels good to the flesh." Again, how confusing this is for many people. We see this when churches put up a rainbow flag, which has somehow been turned into symbolism, representing this idea of fleshly desires and saying, "It is okay to do what you feel for yourself." All I have ever known the rainbow to represent is a promise from God that He would never flood the earth again with water. This is a biblical fact. Also, the word *pride* means a deep satisfaction from one's own achievements, a consciousness of one's own dignity, or being proud of a particular quality or skill. A person can have too much pride or not any at all. It's unbelievable how the original meanings of these words were allowed to be changed, because a few decided they would suddenly have new definitions. Again, that's how this world today has conformed to a few changes by putting individuals first and Jesus second.

Genesis 9:12–17—And God said, "This is the sign of the covenant I am making between me and you and every living creature with you, a covenant for all generations to come. I have set my rainbow in the clouds, and it will be the sign of the covenant between me and the earth. Whenever I bring clouds over the earth and the rainbow appears in the clouds, I will remember my covenant between me and you and all the living creatures of every kind. Never again will the waters become a flood to destroy all life.

Proverbs 11:2—When pride comes, then comes disgrace, but with the humble is wisdom.

However, I have been listening and watching pastors for some time now, and I have only been able to find a few who will just come right out and say it like it is. That is also very sad to me. They kind of just go around the topics, hinting at the problem. Well, I'm not going around it. God's Word says it plainly. Participating in same-sex relationships is a sin like any other sin. As far as transgender sex changes, a person is literally taking the God-given sex they were born with from God and defying His creation. God created everyone and loves everyone the same, exactly as they are, without any changes. This has nothing to do with the demeanor of these people. Some of the kindest people I know are in same-sex relationships, and some say they have also accepted Christ as their Savior or so they believe. Like I stated earlier, if someone has actually accepted Christ in their heart as their Lord and Savior, they would experience a change. Of course, any addiction is not right in the eyes of the Lord. I have had some people say to me, "Why don't you ask Jesus why he made me this way?" My answer to that is simply that Jesus did not make you a certain way. When Adam and Eve chose their desires over God, that is when our world became a fallen world. Every individual born into this world since then is broken, in one way or another, so no one person is the exception. Jesus doesn't look at us the same way we look at ourselves. He only looks at our heart. He knows when you have made the decision to choose yourself over Him. This is not about how kind someone is, and it is not about loving others. Again, Jesus said, "Love first"; He didn't say, "Agree first." Also, when you have accepted Jesus as your Lord and Savior, and you truly know the Word and that the Word is Jesus, you are changed to a new person and will want to be more Christlike each day and will, therefore, not want to indulge in those same desires. Beyond them believing they have accepted Christ, they have no real understanding of God's Word, except what others have told them. These people that have previously accepted Christ are being held in captivity by their sin. If they truly accepted Christ, then, they will go to Heaven; but again, if you are knowledgeable in God's Word, then, you know there is heaven and there is also the Kingdom. Our Jesus is enough to remove these fleshly desires, but a person must put their faith in Him to do this. The question is, "How much does the person really want to remove these desires?"

1 John 4:19–21—We love because He first loved us. Whoever claims to love God yet hates a brother or sister is a liar. For whoever does not love their

brother and sister, whom they have seen, cannot love God, whom they have not seen. And He has given us this command: Anyone who loves God must also love their brother and sister.

It's okay to disagree with others, but we should also share with them why we disagree. Knowing this is in God's Word makes me concerned for those who say they are saved, but then participate in these acts of sin continually and/or promote these behaviors. If one is truly saved, and knows this is stated in the Word, then, one would not have a desire to make these choices, because they would want to be as Christlike as possible. Even though we as Christians, saved by grace, do fall sometimes, we get back up and start again and take ourselves out of those types of situations, and we keep Jesus in our daily lives. We have the Holy Spirit inside of us to help us when we start to mess up and make these decisions. Many say, "It's just the way they are" or "They were born like that." This is not true, because God didn't create anyone to be a sinner. God wants good for all of us who choose Him, and it cannot be both ways. All people have certain impulses or temptations, but it is the decision to act on them that makes the difference. That is a choice they make. It is also sad to hear people say that someone cannot love them if they don't accept them for who they are and what they are doing. This is not true! I know for a fact that you can love someone with your whole heart and not agree with their choices, because I love some people with my whole heart and don't agree with them.

However, some people struggle more than others because they are full of pride and have become convinced that they should only think of themselves. Well, the world is full of people who are always trying to convince others that it is only about them and, as stated before, will tell them what they choose is okay. Those people are also lost. They may have accepted Jesus as their Savior, but Jesus is the Word. So, how can someone believe in Jesus but not the Word? It just doesn't make any sense. Many people have had experiences in their life that have made a huge impact on them in a negative way. When this happens, they just decide to disregard their previous life and choose to only please themselves. It's a blame game that makes them feel better when life didn't go the way they planned. This is exactly what Satan wants. Remember, Satan is not in Hell. Hell is reserved for him as stated in the Book of Revelations in the Bible. He roams the earth with one intention. That intention is to take as many individuals as possible away from Christ. The sad reality is that many people had a full life with Christ (if they had already accepted Him as their Savior), and with people who loved them and still do; but, because they chose to listen to others and the world and to disregard the Word, they are now more lost than they were previously. Remember, when you accept Jesus as your Savior, you are also accepting Him as your Lord.

Ephesians 5:1–6—Therefore be imitators of God, as beloved children. And walk in love, as Christ loved us and gave himself up for us, a fragrant offering and sacrifice to God. But sexual immorality, and all impurity or covetousness must not even be named among you, as is proper among saints. Let there be no filthiness nor foolish talk nor crude joking, which are out of place, but instead let there be thanksgiving. For you may be sure of this, that everyone who is sexually immoral or impure, or who is covetous (that is, an idolater), has no inheritance in the kingdom of Christ and God. Let no one deceive you with empty words, for because of these things the wrath of God comes upon the sons of disobedience.

John 3:36—Whoever believes in the Son has eternal life; whoever does not obey the Son shall not see life, but the wrath of God remains on him.

1 John 2:4—If someone claims, "I know God," but doesn't obey God's commandments, that person is a liar and is not living in the truth.

Romans 6:23—For the wages of sin is death, but the gift of God is eternal life in Christ Jesus our Lord.

[13]

HE IS WHERE OUR HELP COMES FROM

I KNOW OF PEOPLE that have fought their fleshly desires and chose to go to God in prayer and asked for help from the Holy Spirit, who came into their heart when they accepted Jesus as their Lord and Savior. I also know of others who have indulged in some type of immoral sexual lifestyle because they weren't saved but have since been saved through grace and are no longer making those choices. There are multiple organizations which you can search and find that are made up of people who have chosen Jesus over their previous lifestyle choices. Some of these groups are simply trying to defend the rights of those who formerly were in same-sex relationships, but have since accepted Christ and repented and are now trying their best to live by God's Word daily. They themselves will tell you it is a choice they have made. Hallelujah!

Ezekiel 3:18–21—If I warn the wicked saying, "You are under the penalty of death, but you fail to deliver the warning, they will die in their sins. And I will hold you responsible for their deaths. If you warn them and they refuse to repent and keep on sinning, they will die in their sins. But you will have saved yourself because you obeyed me.

Romans 13:1–14—Let every person be subject to the governing authorities. For there is no authority except from God, and those that exist have been instituted by God. Therefore, whoever resists the authorities resists what God has appointed, and those who resist will incur judgement. For rulers are not a terror to good conduct, but instead to bad. Would you have no fear of the one who is in authority? Then do what is good, and you will receive his approval, for he is God's servant for your good. But if you do wrong, be afraid, for he does not bear the sword in vain. For he is the servant of God, an avenger who carries out God's wrath on the wrongdoer. Therefore, one must be in subjection, not only to avoid God's wrath, but also for the sake of conscience. For because of this, you also pay taxes, for the authorities are ministers of God, attending to this very thing. Pay to all what is owed to them: taxes to whom taxes are owed, revenue to whom revenue is owed, respect to whom respect is owed, honor to whom honor is owed. Owe no one anything, except to love each other, for the one who loves another has fulfilled the law. For the commandments, you shall not commit adultery, you shall not murder, you shall not steal, you shall not covet, and any other commandment, are summed up in this word: You shall love your neighbor as yourself. Love does no wrong to a neighbor; therefore, love is the fulfilling of the law. Besides this, you know the time, that the hour has come for you to wake from sleep. For salvation is nearer to us now than we first believed. The night is far gone; the day is at hand. So, then let us cast off the works of darkness and put on the armor of light. Let us walk properly as in the daytime, not in orgies or drunkenness, not in sexual immorality and sensuality, not in quarreling and jealousy. But put on the Lord Jesus Christ, and make no provision for the flesh, to gratify its desires.

Again, no one is perfect. Only the Lord is perfect. However, it is a great thing to try our best to live as He wants us to, and when we slip up, we know He is there to catch us. Hallelujah for Grace!

[14]

BE PREPARED

YOU SEE NOW THAT a lot of people believe what they are doing is okay, especially if no one tells them otherwise, or if God's Word is not in their decision-making process. The decisions we make should involve the wonderful and powerful Word of God. This is the voice of truth for how we should live our lives each day. We need to share it with as many others as we possibly can, because as it states, "He will come like a thief in the night."

1 Thessalonians 5:2—for you know very well that the day of the Lord will come like a thief in the night

Luke 4:19—to proclaim the year of the Lord's favor (this means when He is ready to receive sinners coming to him)

Matthew 24:43–44—But know this, that if the master of the house had known in what part of the night "the thief was coming, he would have stayed awake and would not have let his house be broken into." Therefore, you also must be "ready, for the Son of Man is coming at an hour you do not expect."

Matthew 4:17—From that time Jesus began to preach, "Repent of your sins and turn to God, for the Kingdom of Heaven is near."

Matthew 7:21–23—Not everyone who says to me, "Lord, Lord," will enter the Kingdom of Heaven, but the one who does the will of my Father who is in heaven. On that day, many will say to me, "Lord, Lord, did we not prophesy in your name, and cast out demons in your name, and do many mighty works in your name?" And then I will declare to them, "I never knew you; depart from me, you workers of lawlessness."

Revelation 3:3—Go back to what you heard and believed at first; hold to it firmly. Repent and turn to me again. If you don't wake up, I will come to you suddenly, as unexpected as a thief.

Where do you want to go when He comes? Don't you want your family and friends with you? Doesn't that matter to you?

John 12:48—But all who reject me and my message, will be judged on the day of judgement by the truth I have spoken.

That's why I'm so confused about Christians agreeing with choices that their friends are making.

Don't you want those friends with you when Jesus returns? Isn't it worth having the conversation with them about the Good News that is offered freely to all of us? I would think, as a Christian, that you would even experience sadness to know they wouldn't be with you. Your friends need you to not only love them, but to be honest with them, even if it means they may leave you for the time being. So many young people are all about their friends, and if their friends are Christians and they hear this from them, they could be reassured that there is another choice. That choice is Christ! The Gospel makes a way for everyone; a way when it seems there is no way. We must share this message!

[15]

OH, HOLY SPIRIT COME

GOD CHOSE US BY being our creator, and He has hopes that all of us will choose Him by accepting His son Jesus as our Lord and Savior. Remember, He did not create anyone to be a sinner. God's Word does not say that, just because you ask Jesus in your heart to be your Lord and Savior, you can then sin repeatedly knowing you are saved. The truth is that, when you truly accept Him, and the Holy Spirit fills you, a change will take place within you. This change is so powerful that you will no longer have a desire to do ungodly things but, instead, you will want to pursue God and walk in His Word the best you can every day. Even if a person struggles with a certain desire, they have Jesus to help them now. The Holy Spirit is there to help each person fight their battles. Sometimes, many people who accepted Christ when they were younger begin to push back the voice of the Holy Spirit with the sounds and voices of the world. The truth is that if someone did accept Christ as their Lord and Savior, then the Holy Spirit dwells inside of them and is just waiting for that person to reach out to him. So many people forget about the Holy Spirit, the Comforter, as He is referred to by Jesus. Since Jesus died for our sins on the cross, and rose on the third day to sit at the right hand of the Father in Heaven, he promised us that the Holy Spirit would remain in our hearts when we accepted Him. He is also referred to as the Holy Ghost, the spirit that dwells in our hearts to help us throughout our life on Earth. He is a part of the Trinity (three in one), God the Father, God the Son (Jesus), and the Holy Ghost.

2 Corinthians 3:17—Now the Lord is the Spirit, and where the Spirit of the Lord is, there is freedom.

1 Corinthians 6:19-20—Do you not know that your bodies are temples of the Holy Spirit, who is in you, whom you have received from God? You are not your own; you were bought at a price. Therefore, honor God with your bodies.

John 14:16—And I will ask the Father, and he will give you another advocate to help you and be with you forever.

John 14:26—But the Advocate, the Holy Spirit, whom the Father will send in my name, will teach you all things and will remind you of everything I have said to you.

Acts 1:8—Jesus said to his disciples, "But you will receive power when the Holy Spirit comes on you; and you will be my witnesses in Jerusalem, and in all Judea and Samaria, and to the ends of the earth.

Ezekiel 36:27—And I will put my Spirit in you and move you to follow my decrees and be careful to keep my laws.

1 Corinthians 2:11—For who knows a person's thoughts except their own spirit within them? In the same way no one knows the thoughts of God except the Spirit of God.

[16]

EXPERIENCING BAPTISM

BECAUSE OF THIS AMAZING joy you now feel from accepting Christ, getting baptized is another step that you will want to do. Again, many people are confused by baptism. *Baptism* is an outward way to publicly show others about the grace that you have received. When you are put beneath the water, it represents dying with Christ and dying to your old self. When you rise out of the water, it represents rising as Christ did from the grave to your new self. The old is gone and the new has come! You are outwardly showing others that you have accepted Jesus Christ as your Savior and Lord. To repeat, when you truly accept Jesus into your heart, you will want to be baptized! You will want to show others that you have received the grace of Jesus Christ and are born again!

Acts 2:38—And Peter said to them, "Repent and be baptized every one of you in the name of Jesus

Christ for the forgiveness of your sins, and you will receive the gift of the Holy Spirit."

1 Peter 3:21—And this water is a picture of baptism, which now saves you, not by removing dirt from your body, but as a response to God from a clean conscience. It is effective because of the resurrection of Jesus Christ.

Acts 22:16—And now why do you wait? Rise and be baptized and wash away your sins, calling on his name.

Colossians 2:12—having been buried with him in baptism, in which you were also raised with him through faith in the powerful working of God, who raised him from the dead

Galatians 3:27—For as many of you as were baptized into Christ have put on Christ

Luke 3:16—(This verse is John the Baptist explaining his baptizing of people before he baptizes Jesus) John answered them all, saying, "I baptize you with water, but he who is mightier that I is coming, the strap of whose sandals I am not worthy to untie. He will baptize you with the Holy Spirit and fire.

Mark 16:16—Whoever believes and is baptized will be saved, but whoever does not believe will be condemned.

Matthew 28:19—Go ye therefore, and teach all nations, baptizing them in the name of the Father, and of the Son, and of the Holy Ghost (This is Jesus's Great Commission to the disciples)

[17]

THREE IN ONE

PEOPLE TODAY WHO I refer to as "being lost at the present time" are either those who have never known Jesus and the Word or those who have strayed from the Lord. They have chosen to listen to others and to the world and have pushed away the Holy Spirit and the Word. When battling the lust of the eye, the lust of the flesh, or the pride of life, a person should run to God the Father, God the Son (Jesus), and the Holy Ghost (Spirit). They are three in one! Sometimes they are referred to as the *Trinity*. Remember, once a person is saved through grace, the Holy Spirit is inside of their heart, so they can take their struggles to Him and He will speak to the Lord. This will help them overcome those desires. When you are saved, Jesus wants to be included in all parts of your life, not just the valleys. Reach out to Him every day and thank Him for your blessings, and then bless Him for all He has done for you. God rewards you when He knows you are trying your best to walk with Him.

Hebrews 11:6—And without faith, it is impossible to please God, because anyone who comes to Him must believe that He exists and that He rewards those who earnestly seek Him.

Matthew 6:33—But seek ye first the Kingdom of God and His righteousness, and all these things will be added to you.

Proverbs 3:6—In all your ways acknowledge Him, and He will make straight your paths.

A very good example of this in the Word is when Paul struggles with the sin inside of him even after he has accepted Christ as his savior and Lord. Paul shares this in the Book of Romans.

As Paul states:

Romans 7:15–25—I do not understand what I do. For what I want to do, I do not do, but what I hate I do. And if I do what I do not want to do, I agree that the law is good. As it is, it is no longer I myself who do it, but it is sin living in me. I know that nothing good lives in me, that is, in my sinful nature. For I have the desire to do what is good, but I cannot carry it out. For what I do is not the good I want to do; no, the evil I do not want to do—this I keep on doing. Now if I do what I do not want to do, it is no longer I who do it, but it is sin living in me that does it. So, I find this law at work: When I want to do good, evil is right there with me. For in my inner being, I delight in God's law; but I see another law at work in the members of my body, waging war against the law of my mind and making me a prisoner of the law of sin at work within my members. What a wretched man I am! Who will rescue me from this body of death? Thanks be to God—through Jesus Christ our Lord!

Paul is saying that we all struggle with our fleshly desires, even after we become Christians; but, if we close the door to those desires by completely separating ourselves from them and going to the Spirit with those desires we struggle with, the Spirit will take our struggles to Jesus and the desires will begin to fade. No one is immune to this, even after being saved. Our spirit is saved, but our flesh is not. That is why we have our struggles, but we can defeat those desires and struggles with the help of God, Jesus, and the Holy Spirit once we are saved. Otherwise, we do not have any help. The question is: Do we really want help?

Proverbs 22:4—The reward for humility and fear of the Lord is riches and honor and life.

[18]
PERSONAL EXPERIENCES

I AM LIVING PROOF that I would not be where I am today if I had not had the Holy Spirit within me to comfort me and guide me to the Word. When I was eleven, I went through a confirmation class in a Methodist church. It was something that children just did in the Methodist church, because they were supposedly of an age that they could understand the story of Christ and what it means for Him to be your Savior. For me, I did understand that, but I really did not have a personal relationship with Jesus until I was much older. We did not attend church regularly when I was older, so it wasn't often on my mind to go to the Word when I needed guidance. When I married and had children of my own, I began to attend church and Sunday school regularly, as I mentioned earlier. I rededicated my life to Christ when my oldest child accepted Him as her Lord and

Savior at age nine. The more I included Jesus and the Word in my life, the more I felt the Holy Spirit move inside of me. After the divorce, it was the Holy Spirit that kept me going every day. Life was hard, but He always got me through it one step at a time. I felt the Holy Spirit with me at work, at home, and every night when I went to bed. I really went deeper into the Word after all my children were grown and out of the house. I thought the worst days were over for a while. Then, we had a family member stray from the Lord and choose their self over Jesus. They chose to surround their self with others who either were not believers or who just put their self in front of Christ. Again, if you truly know Jesus, then you know the Word, and you know what is right with God and what is not right with God. It's as simple as that. Blaming Jesus, and saying it was Him that made you a certain way, is also not okay. Every person has their own issues and struggles, but Jesus wants to see if you will choose Him and not yourself. It is not okay to pick out pieces of God's Word that you want to believe and, then, disregard the other parts to try and defend your choices. I literally cried for endless nights in a row as did my other immediate family members and, again, the Holy Spirit's presence was felt intensely. The Holy Spirit is who got me through each day. On top of that, we were saddened by the fact that some of our relatives were okay with this family member straying from Christ. Some of their words were, "We just want them to be happy" and "What if we are wrong about what the Bible says?" I couldn't believe it! I thought I knew these relatives so well, when I clearly did not. Also, they obviously did not know me well at all. These are people that I had known my entire life. I replied, "WHAT? We are not wrong about what the Bible says." The Bible is the Word, and the Word is Jesus, God the Father, and the Holy Spirit. Therefore, there is no way it can be wrong. The thought that this statement was even vocalized really made me concerned for some of my relatives. This created a huge break in relationships within the family. It's hard to lose family because you stand firm in your faith, but if you don't stand firm in your faith, then you won't stand for anything.

Then, there are people who have said to me, "If God is real and is such a good God as others say He is, and I have tried to be the best person I can be and am also kind, He will surely let me come into Heaven." My reply to that statement was, "Then why did He send His Son Jesus?" There would have been no reason for Jesus to be sent by His Father, God Almighty, to come here if we could just be nice enough and still go to Heaven. Jesus Christ came to this earth to die for our sins, and He is the ONLY way to the Father in

Heaven. This is always a statement that proceeds to make people think about their original comment on getting into Heaven. Also, when someone questions the authenticity of Jesus Christ, I simply ask them, "In what year were you born?" Then, when they reply with a particular year, I just ask them, "Was that BC or AD, before Christ or after the Death of Christ?" You see, our entire timeline is based around the life of Jesus. People also don't have a response after that statement either. Jesus was here and did walk on this earth and was real beyond a shadow of a doubt!

Lastly, there are people who just will not bring themselves to hear the Word of God because they are afraid it is real and, then, they would have to admit that the behaviors and actions they have allowed to take control of their lives are not aligned with the Word. Instead, they refer to believers as a "cult." That just shows they have no idea what a cult is. The word *cult* is a term that does not refer to religion but to a social movement. Again, it gives people an excuse for the choices they have made, and those choices were made because they chose themselves over Christ or they have never been exposed to Christ yet.

[19]

CHOOSING JESUS

I have to say to this day, "I don't know how anyone makes it through difficult times without having Jesus as their Lord and Savior." We all make choices during our lifetime with some being easier than others. What is ultimately the most important thing we can do is choose Jesus over ourselves, our pride, our lust for the eye, and our lust for the flesh. Choosing Jesus doesn't mean that our life will be easy and free of problems. In fact, it is often the opposite, especially in today's world where there are so many religions and atheists, and many worldly temptations. In several Scriptures in the Word, Jesus said, "We (Christians) would face hard times because we have chosen Him."

2 Timothy 3:12—Indeed, all who desire to live a godly life in Christ Jesus will be persecuted.

Matthew 5:10–11—Blessed are those who are persecuted because of righteousness, for theirs is the kingdom of heaven. Blessed are you when people insult you, persecute you and falsely say all kinds of evil against you because of me.

Revelation 2:10—Be faithful, even to the point of death, and I will give you the crown of life.

Some of the toughest situations that a person faces are those that involve family. I truly love every member of my family, but this isn't about love. It's about choosing joy and surrounding yourself with those that believe in Christ and the Word, because it helps strengthen our Christian walk. I can love others that are not like me, even if they are presently lost and searching for something more. It gives me opportunity to witness to them. But I do not surround myself each day with those that are choosing themselves over Christ on a continuous basis, because we do become what we surround ourselves with frequently.

Repeating what I said earlier, "It's not okay to pick and choose what parts of the Word you believe and what parts of the Word you don't." It's all truth and provides a guide for how we should try to live our lives. It has answers to all the questions we face in our lifetime. Honestly, I want to be on the first bus out to the Kingdom when Jesus returns, if I haven't already gone to be with Him.

The Good News is everyone can choose Jesus! There is nothing that people could ever do in their life to keep Jesus from loving them and forgiving them. Some people think they are not good enough and have made too many mistakes and wrong choices. This is not possible with Jesus. He is just waiting for you to choose Him over yourself!

Just imagine how amazing it will be one day to live with Christ in Heaven and maybe even the Kingdom, and your friends and family will hopefully be there with you!

If you are a young person, an adult (younger or older), or even a company/business, I hope you haven't given in to the things of this world just so someone won't be upset with you or just because you don't think your business will do as well. There are so many businesses that have become more successful when they put Jesus at the forefront—and individuals who have discovered their potential once they aligned their life with the Word. If you are a person who is struggling with ungodly desires and you think it's a hopeless situation, please, please, turn to Jesus! He will be there for you! Remember, it doesn't mean that it will be easy, or that you won't have difficult times, but it will be so much better; and, trusting in

Him will continue to make your situation more and more hopeful every day. Surround yourself with believers and submerge yourself in the Word. After all, we become what we surround ourselves with, so let that be our Jesus! Completely humble yourself before God, and you will come out successful.

Remember, all that happens in our life is based on God's timeline, not ours. Sometimes, it is frustrating for us when everything doesn't go our way at the exact time that we believe it should. This is when it's so important to give yourself completely to His will and have faith that He knows what He is doing with your life. How do I know this is true for myself? I did exactly that, and that's how I wrote this book, so I will share the experience with you. I began considering writing a book several years ago, but I put the thought aside and continued moving forward with life. This past year, 2021-2022, I began not sleeping at night for days in a row. I would pray and talk to God about writing a book, and I would ask Him if that was what He wanted me to do. You see, even though I have been a teacher for many years, I have never written a book of any kind and didn't know the first thing about how to do it. Finally, I got tired of not sleeping, sat up in bed at 1:30 a.m. one night and said, "Okay, God, I will do it!" I got up and began typing, and the words just flowed out of me. I didn't even know if

I was typing the correct way and using the correct program, etc. I just typed on a Word document and hoped for the best. I never had trouble sleeping for days in a row after that night. I obviously did not write the book in one night, but I worked on it continuously throughout the year around my time spent at work and time spent with family. I didn't even tell anyone about it. I just knew that I needed to share the Word and Jesus with others. I know now that it was the Holy Spirit that was talking to me, giving me the push that I needed. When I finally decided to let go and follow His lead, I was able to move forward with what He wanted to do for others through me.

It is my hope that you will also want this same mercy and grace that I have with Jesus Christ. If you do want to receive Him into your heart, the following is a prayer that can be used to commit your life to Jesus, but you must truly believe, as Jesus knows every person's heart. You can pray this prayer:

Lord Jesus, I come to you to ask You to forgive me of my sins and to come into my heart. I make You my Lord and Savior and give my whole life to You. I believe with my heart and confess with my mouth that You are the Son of God, and that you died on the cross for my sins and rose on the third day, so that I could receive Your grace and be cleansed by Your blood and made new. In Jesus' mighty name, I pray,

    Amen and Amen

When you have prayed this prayer, please know that you are now a believer and the Holy Spirit dwells inside of you forever. He is there to help you in every way. Submerge yourself in the Word, seek out others who are believers, and find out about baptism. I rejoice with you, for you have made the most important decision in your life! Jesus loves you so much! Even if you aren't completely sure of what the Bible says or what the Scriptures mean, then, please, take the time each day to read and study God's Word. I do believe, with all my heart, that when you do, your eyes will be opened to the truth. You will be amazed at how your life will change!

Now, you can truly be a light to others and guide them toward Christ by sharing the Good News; and what better way to do this than letting them know that you were also lost once but are now created new in Christ? When others witness this change in someone, they begin to feel that it can happen for them also.

Romans 10:9–10—because, if you confess with your mouth that Jesus is Lord and believe in your heart that God raised him from the dead, you will be saved. For with the heart, one believes and is justified, and with the mouth one confesses and is saved.

Hebrews 7:25—Therefore, he is able to save completely those who come to God through Him, because he always lives to intercede for them

Ephesians 2:8–9—For it is by grace that you have been saved through faith. And this is not your own doing; It is the gift of God, not a result of works, so that no one may boast

John 3:16—For God so loved the world, that He gave His only begotten Son, that whoever believes in Him should not perish but have eternal life.

Our Jesus Is Enough and He Loves YOU!

www.ingramcontent.com/pod-product-compliance
Lightning Source LLC
Chambersburg PA
CBHW071319040426
42444CB00009B/2048